Giraffe

Written by Alex Hall

Enslow PUBLISHING

From Head to Hoof

Published in 2025 by Enslow Publishing, LLC
2544 Clinton Street
Buffalo, NY 14224

Written by:
Alex Hall

Edited by:
Rebecca Phillips-Bartlett

Designed by:
Jasmine Pointer

Cataloging-in-Publication Data
Names: Hall, Alex.
Title: Giraffe / Alex Hall.
Description: Buffalo, NY : Enslow Publishing, 2025. | Series: From head to hoof | Includes glossary.
Identifiers: ISBN 9781978541955 (pbk.) | ISBN 9781978541962 (library bound) | ISBN 9781978541979 (ebook)
Subjects: LCSH: Giraffe--Juvenile literature. | Giraffe--Behavior--Juvenile literature.
Classification: LCC QL737.U56 H355 2025 | DDC 599.638--dc23

Manufactured in the United States of America

CPSIA compliance information: Batch #CW25ENS: For further information contact Enslow Publishing LLC at 1-800-398-2504.

Please visit our website, www.enslowpublishing.com. For a free color catalog of all our high-quality books, call toll free 1-800-398-2504 or fax 1-877-980-4454.

Image Credits

All images are courtesy of Shutterstock.com. With thanks to Getty Images, Thinkstock Photo and iStockphoto.

Cover – Independent birds, ARTvektor, Angus Boyd, YummyBuum. Throughout – LivDeco, ARTvektor. 2–3 – LivDeco, Henk Bogaard. 4–5 – Volodymyr Burdiak. 6–7 – Photo_Traveller, Vladimir Turkenich, a_v_d. 8–9 – Kevin Lings, doleesi. 10–11 – aragami12345s, Dallong. 12–13 – GUDKOV ANDREY, MPH Photos. 14–15 – Pyty, tratong. 16–17 – Chaithanya Krishnan, Mees Kuiper. 18–19 – Stacey Ann Alberts, Richard Seeley. 20–21 – T.W. van Urk, MintImages. 22–23 – Athol Abrahams, Anita van den Broek, Mees Kuiper.

Contents

Words that look like **this** can be found in the glossary on page 24.

Giraffe

Giraffes are the tallest animals in the world. Giraffes can grow to over 16 feet (5 m) tall. Giraffes live in dry African grasslands, called savannas. The place an animal or plant lives is called its habitat.

Giraffes are perfectly suited to the challenging savanna habitat. We are going to explore the bodies of giraffes, from the top of their heads to the bottom of their hooves.

Head

Giraffes have horn-like parts on the top of their heads. These are called ossicones. Giraffes are the only animals born with ossicones. Both male and female giraffes have them.

Female giraffe ossicones are usually thin and hairy. Male giraffe ossicones are thick. The top of their ossicones are hairless. Male giraffes use their ossicones to fight. Fighting rubs the hair off over time.

A giraffe's ossicones add power to attacks with their heads.

Eyes

Giraffes have some of the biggest eyeballs of all land mammals. Their eyes are the size of golf balls. These huge eyes help them have very good eyesight.

Giraffes can see movement from up to 1.2 miles (2 km) away. If one giraffe sees danger, other nearby giraffes will look in that direction. Giraffes can see in color. Many other mammals cannot.

Mouth

Giraffes are herbivores. This means they only eat plants. Giraffes have long tongues that they use to reach leaves high up in trees. Their tongues are almost 1 foot (.5 m) long.

Most giraffes' tongues are purple or black. These dark colors protect their tongues from sunburn while giraffes are eating. Their tough tongues let them eat thorny plants without getting hurt.

Neck

Giraffes have long necks. Their necks help them reach the plants that other animals cannot reach. Their necks can be over 6 feet (2 m) long. They are supported by large muscles on their upper backs.

Giraffes also use their necks when fighting other giraffes. They often fight over which giraffe should be in charge. Giraffes swing their necks and use their heads to hit each other. This is called "necking."

Their long necks lead to very powerful hits.

Body

Giraffes have spots and patches all over their bodies. Their yellow and brown colored fur helps them to camouflage themselves in the savanna.

Giraffes live in groups called herds or towers. Giraffes use spot patterns to recognize other giraffes in their herd. Mother giraffes use spot patterns to know which baby is theirs so they can keep them safe.

Different species of giraffes have different spot patterns.

Tail

A giraffe's tail can reach over 6 feet (2 m) long. That is longer than the height of most adult people. This makes it the longest tail of any land mammal!

Giraffes use their tails to stop insects from biting them. They swing their tails around and try to hit insects out of the air before the insects can bite them.

Legs

Giraffes have very long legs. Their long legs allow them to run at speeds of nearly 37 miles (60 km) an hour. However, long legs also mean they must do the splits to reach water.

Giraffes' legs are very powerful. If giraffes are threatened by predators, such as lions or crocodiles, they will kick to protect themselves. A strong giraffe kick can even kill a lion.

Hooves

All animals with hooves are called ungulates.

At the bottom of the giraffe's leg is the hoof. The hoof is made of keratin. Keratin is the same thing that human hair and nails are made of.

Giraffes have cloven hooves. This means each toe is protected by its own bit of hoof. A giraffe's hooves protect their feet from sharp rocks and prickly thorns. They also stop them from sinking into loose sand.

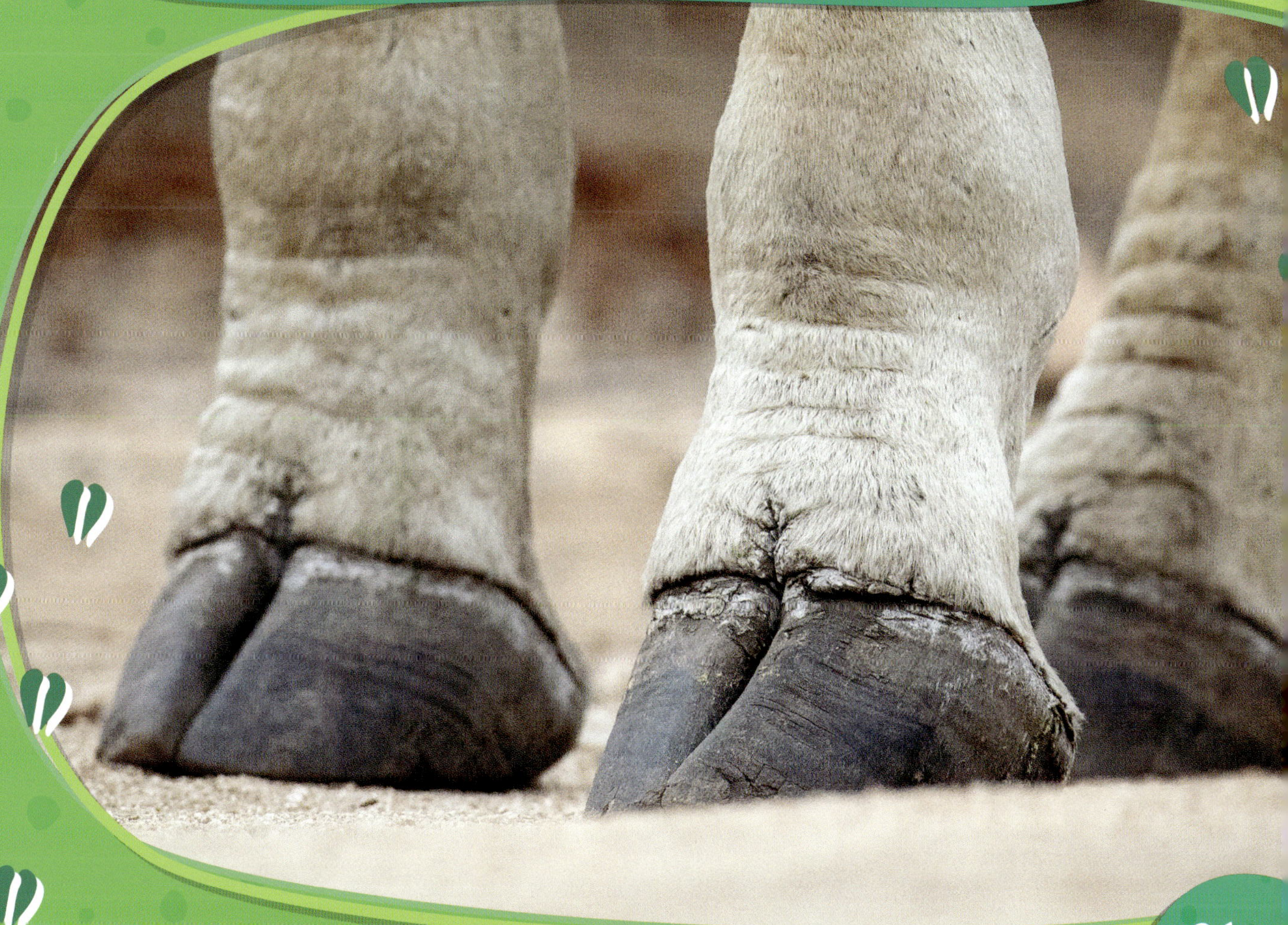

Life Cycle

Giraffes give birth standing up. When they are born, baby giraffes fall 6 feet (2 m) to the ground. Baby giraffes are not hurt when they fall at birth. Baby giraffes are called calves.

Life cycles are the changes living things go through during their lives, leading up to being able to have their own young.

Baby giraffes learn how to stand up soon after being born. They are even able to walk an hour after birth. Giraffes live for around 20 to 25 years.

Glossary

camouflage to blend in with the surroundings

female the sex that can produce offspring or eggs

give birth when a mother creates a baby from her body

insects animals with one or two pairs of wings, six legs, and no backbone

male the sex that fathers offspring

mammals animals that are warm-blooded, have a backbone, and produce milk to feed their children

muscles the parts of the body that move the body around

predators animals that hunt other animals for food

species groups of very similar animals or plants that can create young together

Index